kratts' CREATURES ™

Our Favorite Creatures

by Martin Kratt and Chris Kratt

SCHOLASTIC INC.

New York   Toronto   London   Auckland   Sydney

Exclusive worldwide licensing agent: Momentum Partners, Inc., New York, NY
All graphic maps: Lisa Kelly

cover: *credits to come*
p.4 (clockwise from tl): (c) Fritz Polking/Peter Arnold, Inc.; (c) Gregory G. Dimijian/Photo Researchers, Inc.; (c) Lorne Sulcas/Peter Arnold, Inc.; (c) Peter McDonald/A.N.T. Photo Library; (c) Jeff Lepore/ Photo Researchers, Inc.; (c) Richard Hansen/Photo Researchers, Inc.; (c) Ron & Valerie Taylor/ A.N.T. Photo Library; (c) 1996 Paragon Entertainment Corporation **p.5**: tl: (c) Tom McHugh/ Photo Researcher, Inc.; tc: (c) D. Parer & E. Parer-Cook/AUSCAPE International; tr and bottom: (c) 1996 Paragon Entertainment Corporation **p.6**: (c) Renee Lynn/Photo Researchers, Inc. **p.7**: l: (c) 1996 Paragon Entertainment Corporation; r: (c) Gunter Ziesler/ Peter Arnold, Inc. **p.8**: l: (c) 1996 Paragon Entertainment Corporation; c: (c) Gunter Ziesler/Peter Arnold, Inc.; r: (c) Renee Lynn/Photo Researchers, Inc. **p.9**: l & br: (c) 1996 Paragon Entertainment Corporation; tr: (c) Fritz Polking/Peter Arnold, Inc **p.10**: (c) Y. Arthus-Bertrand/Peter Arnold, Inc. **p.11**: t, bl: (c) Gray Carr Bridgers; br: (c) N.H.P.A./A.N.T. Photo Library **p.12**: (c) Frans Lanting/Minden Pictures **p.13**: all photos (c) Gray Carr Bridgers **p.14**: all photos (c) Frans Lanting/Minden Pictures **p.15**: (c) 1996 Paragon Entertainment Corporation **p.16** (clockwise from tr): (c) Doug Cheeseman/Peter Arnold, Inc.; (c) Luiz C. Marigo/Peter Arnold, Inc.; (c) Gerard Lacz/Peter Arnold, Inc.; (c) Dieter & Mary Plage/Bruce Coleman, Inc.; (c) Silvestris/A.N.T. Photo Libraary **p. 17**: t: (c) 1996 Paragon Entertainment Corporation; c: (c) Lorne Sulcas/Peter Arnold, Inc.; b: (c) Ronald Seitre/Peter Arnold, Inc.
pp.18-20: all photos (c) 1996 Paragon Entertainment Corporation **p.21**: t: (c) 1991 Kennan Ward/DRK Photo; c&b: (c) 1996 Paragon Entertainment Corporation **pp.22-23**: all photos (c) 1996 Paragon Entertainment Corporation **p.24**: t: Eric Robertson/(c) Paragon Entertainment Corporation **p.25**: tl & bottom photos: (c) Eric Robertson; tr: (c) William H. Mullians/Photo Researchers, Inc **pp.26-28**: all photos: (c) 1996 Paragon Entertainment Corporation **p. 29**: t: (c) Gregory G. Dimijian/Phtoto Researchers, Inc.; b: (c) 1996 Paragon Entertainment Corporation **p.30**: t&bl: (c) 1996 Paragon Entertainment Corporation; br: (c) G.C. Kelley/Photo Researchers, Inc. **p.31**: all photos: (c) 1996 Paragon Entertainment Corporation **p.32**: t: (c) G.D. Anderson/A.N.T.Photo Library; b: (c) 1996 Paragon Entertainment Corporation **p.33**: (c) 1996 Paragon Entertainment Corporation **p.34**: (c) D. Parer & E. Parer-Cook/ AUSCAPE International **p.35**: all photos: (c) 1996 Paragon Entertainment Coroporation **p.36**: t: (c) 1996 Paragon Entertainment Corporation; b: (c) Roland Seitre/Peter Arnold, Inc. **p.37**: t: (c) A.N.T.; b: (c) 1996 Paragon Entertainment Corporation **p.38**: t: (c) 1996 Paragon Entertainment Corporation; c: (c) Dave Watts/A.N.T. b: (c) Photo Researchers, Inc. **p.39**: all photos: (c) 1996 Paragon Entertainment Corporation **p.40**: c: (c) Eric Robertson; bl: (c) William Kratt; br: (c) Linda Kratt **p.41**: l: (c) Eric Robertson r: (c) Jeff Lepore/Photo Researchers, Inc. **p.42**: (c) 1996 Paragon Entertainment Corporation **p.43**: (c) Marty Cordano/DRK Photo **p.44**: t: (c) Ron & Valerie Taylor/A.N.T.; b: (c) 1996 Paragon Entertainment Corporation **p.45**: t&c: (c) 1996 Paragon Entertainment Corporation; b: (c) Kelvin Aitken/A.N.T. **p.46**: clockwise from tl: (c) E.R. Degginger/Animals Animals; (c) Peter Parks/Animals Animals; (c) E.R. Degginger/Earth Scenes; (c) E.R. Degginger/Earth Scenes **p.47**: clockwise from tl: (c) Fran Lanting/Minden Pictures; (c) John Giustina/The Wildlife Collection; (c) 1996 Paragon Entertainment Corporation; (c) Jack Swenson/The Wildlife Collection; (c) Tom McHugh/Photo Researchers, Inc.; (c) John Giustina/The Wildlife Collection; center: (c) 1996 Paragon Entertainment Corporation **p.48**: (c) 1996 Paragon Entertainment Corporation

ISBN 0-590-53744-X

Copyright © 1996 by Paragon Entertainment Corporation.
Kratts' Creatures ® and Ttark are registered trademarks of Paragon Entertainment Corporation.
All rights reserved. Published by Scholastic Inc.

Book design by Todd Lefelt

12 11 10 9 8 7 6 5 4 3 2 1   6 7 8 9/9 0 1/0

Printed in the U.S.A.
First Scholastic printing, October 1996

To all the cool creatures we share the planet with
(Of course that includes Mom and Dad)

Cheetah

Giraffe

Rhino

Warthog

Macaw

Wombat

Reef Shark

Wolf

Going off on wildlife adventures is exciting! You meet all kinds of funny, bizarre, fascinating, weird, and wonderful creatures. Sometimes you have to hike high up in the mountains, dive deep in the ocean, or camp out in the icy cold to meet up with the animals. But that's not the hardest part of going on a wildlife adventure. The toughest part is trying to decide of all the creatures you've met, which is your favorite. After all there are so many cool creatures to choose from. Have you ever met the...

Black Bear

Bent-Wing Bat

Chimpanzee

Chris

Martin

Cheetah

Meet the Speedster of the Savanna!

… The Fastest Creature on Land!

… The Colossally Charismatic!

… CHEETAH! ! !

If you want to check out cheetahs, Africa is the place to be! Africa has HUGE open areas of grassland savanna — and that's what cheetahs like best. We started our search for the ultimate speed demon … in the country called Kenya …

...and that's exactly where we found them.

... and that's exactly where we found them.

How FAST *is* a cheetah?!

A Cheetah can reach top speeds of 71 miles per hour!!

That's...

- faster than a Thompson gazelle (50 mph)

- faster than a grizzly bear (30 mph)

- faster than a timber wolf (40 mph)

- faster than an Olympic runner (27 mph)

- faster than the Kentucky Derby's champion racehorse (43.3 mph)

- faster than your mom drives on the highway (55 mph)

But how *can* cheetahs run so fast?

The Cheetah Running Arsenal
special features of this great sprinting machine

Super-flexible backbone

precision tail balance

Strong claws

light, slender body frame

- Super-flexible backbone: can bend and flex like a spring! So the cheetah can take super-long 23-foot strides!!

- Precision tail balance: helps the cheetah make high speed turns. He uses his tail for balance like you use your arms on a balance beam.

- Strong claws: cheetahs have thick, strong claws for super traction. Imagine how much traction you would have if you had cheetah claws on your sneakers!

- Light, slender body frame: the lighter the frame, the faster you go! A cheetah is a lean, mean, sprinting machine!!

These features help a cheetah run down its favorite prey... gazelles. And I have some firsthand experience of the running machine in action... from the gazelle's perspective.

Robbie was an orphaned cheetah, but full grown when Martin and I met him. We took him out to the savanna for a run.

When I started jogging, Robbie's predator instinct kicked in. He was watching me. Robbie was tuned in to every move I made. And I felt like a gazelle being watched by my most feared predator.

I started running faster.

Robbie sprang into action. He picked up speed in a flash. I ran as fast as I could possibly run and made turns to try to shake him. Robbie's tail was whipping around, keeping him balanced as he picked up more and more speed. His strides were getting longer and longer. Robbie was gaining on me.

I didn't have a chance. I looked over my shoulder as Robbie's paw reached up. He grabbed my hip. He tripped me up and I went down in a cloud of dust. When I looked up, Robbie was standing over me. He was looking down at me and, if Robbie could speak English, I'm sure he would have said "Gotcha!" Now I know what it's like being a gazelle and being chased by the fastest land creature on Earth! With me, Robbie was just playing. But for a gazelle, it's the real thing!

If you're walking around Africa and you hear a chirp, it may not be a bird.... It might be a cheetah!! Cheetahs chirp! That's how a mom calls her cubs together.

It's amazing! She sounds like a bird. Wait a second. Maybe the Cheetah isn't really our absolute favorite. How about ...

The Macaw

Red and Green Macaws

These cool creatures are the spectacularly stunning macaws of South America!!

Scarlet Macaw

We went to Peru to check them out. We had a real creature mystery on our hands because macaws do something *very, very* strange....

Can you tell the difference between a scarlet macaw and a red and green macaw? Here's a hint: Look closely at the color patterns on the wing. The scarlet macaw has a row of yellow feathers and the red and green macaw doesn't.

Macaws eat clay!!!! But why?!!

A claylick is a place where macaws eat clay! Every morning, the macaws gather at their favorite claylick along the river. However, there are predators, like ocelots and snakes, at the claylicks. That means macaws have to be very, very cautious.

How to Get Close to a Cautious Flock of Clay-eating Macaws
(in 3 easy steps)

1) cover yourself with clay from head to toe

2) lie down on a mudbank

3) think like clay, feel like clay, try to *be* clay

If you're lucky, the macaws will think you are just part of the claylick. We had to wait at the claylick for three or four hours! Finally, the macaws came down to eat!

Look at these macaws munching on clay. They're eating clay like it was candy! Macaws use their feet a lot like we use our hands. Their feet can even reach their mouths! Imagine being able to eat with your feet instead of your hands!!

But WHY!! WHY on earth do macaws eat clay!?!!

Three Theories for Why Macaws Eat Clay

1) <u>Clay neutralizes the poison in plant seeds!</u> Macaws eat the seeds of fruits and berries. Some of the seeds have poison in them. Scientists think that the clay helps cancel out the poison so the macaws don't get sick!

2) <u>Clay has minerals!</u> Macaws might eat clay because it has minerals like calcium, potassium, and sodium in it! So a macaw eats clay just like you eat daily vitamin tablets!

3) <u>Clay tastes good!</u> Macaws might just eat clay because they like the taste of it. It's the same reason I eat chocolate cake!

Nobody knows which theory is correct. It could be all three!!
The macaws are very cool, but what about . . .

The Rhinoceros

We like rhinos because they remind us of all those prehistoric mammals that once roamed the world — the mastodons, saber-toothed cats, cave bears, and the woolly rhinos. Those animals are gone now — but the rhino is still here!

He's just so prehistoric-looking!!

There are five different species of rhinos living in the world today.

BLACK RHINO

INDIAN RHINO

WHITE RHINO

JAVAN RHINO

SUMATRAN RHINO

We were just hanging out in Africa looking for rhinos. We knew we were close when Martin fell into a rhino midden. (That's the place where a rhino goes to the bathroom.) We ended up finding both of the African species, the black rhino and the white rhino. What's the difference?? Here's how you tell:

Black rhino: narrow lips, weighs up to 3002 pounds, dark gray color

White rhino: wide lips, weighs up to 4982 pounds, slate gray to yellow-brown color

One thing that both species have in common is their horns. And that's the same reason that both species are threatened with extinction. People called poachers hunt and kill them for their horns. Today, many governments are working to protect rhinos from poachers, which is great, because rhinos are definitely some of our favorite creatures. But then again, how about the...

Chimpanzees

Chimpanzees! We'll never forget the time we hung out with three orphan chimps in Africa.

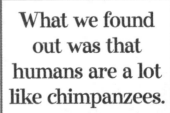

What we found out was that humans are a lot like chimpanzees.

Sophie, Naika, and Tess were three very young chimps who had lost their families and didn't know much about being wild chimps. We had a lot to learn, too, so the five of us spent a day in the woods trying to live like wild chimps. They would teach us what they knew and we would teach them a few things, too!

Chris
3 years old

Naika
2.5 years old

Martin
3 years old

Tess
2 years old

Sophie
4 years old

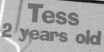

The first thing we found out was that chimps love to play.

They wrestle!

They tumble!

They run around!

And they love to be tickled. When we tickled Sophie, she laughed!

They swing from trees!

Chimps make lots of faces. They communicate with each other with different faces, and this is the chimpanzee language that we learned:

Upset

Afraid

Playful

This is what Naika's face looked like when she sat on an anthill. . . .

She screamed. She freaked out. She waved her arms around and ran in circles. The ants were all over her, biting hard! She didn't know what to do. We were chasing around after her trying to help. Then finally she jumped into Martin's arms and started pointing to where the ants were biting her. We helped pick them out.

After that, Naika was pretty sleepy, but where was she going to sleep? She had never had a chance to learn how to build a nest like wild chimpanzees do, so. . . we taught her!

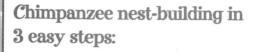

Chimpanzee nest-building in 3 easy steps:

1) Find a nice tree with a fork in it.

2) Pull leafy branches back into nest area.

3) Sit in nest, pack down, and make comfortable.

That's one of the really incredible things about chimps. They are tool-using animals just like humans are! Wild chimps use long pieces of grass to fish for termites, and they use rocks and sticks to break open nuts. We taught these tricks to Sophie and she learned each one in less than two minutes!

That's smart. The reason that chimps and humans can use tools is because we both have hands with opposable thumbs. Opposable thumbs are thumbs that can touch the tips of other fingers. They are really good for grabbing things. And chimps have an extra bonus — they have two more opposable thumbs on their *feet.* Imagine being able to do everything *you* do with your hands with your *feet;* things like brushing your teeth and writing a letter.

Here are some other things chimps and humans have in common:

Chimps are social.
In the wild they live in big family groups called troops, and they take care of each other.

Chimps appreciate good grooming.
Chimps like to sit around and pick ticks off of each other. After they pick them they eat them. One time Naika got a little confused and thought Martin's birthmark was a tick. She started digging into it with her fingernail, trying to get it off!

Chimps like to share.
When we had snacks of figs and nuts the chimps wouldn't eat everything themselves, they SHARED! I couldn't believe it when Tess offered me a piece of fig. She just stuck it in my face! And when she wanted a nut that I had, she asked for it with the chimp "share face" and "share sound."

No doubt about it, chimps and humans are a lot alike in the way we look and act. Can you tell these guys apart?

Did you know that 98 percent of our DNA (genetic material) is the same as that of chimps?

Another thing we always liked about chimpanzees was their hairstyle. Hey, remember that other black-haired animal that taught us a few things… about camping?!?

The Black Bear

We had our first great wildlife adventure with a black bear in the Adirondack Mountains of New York State, USA.

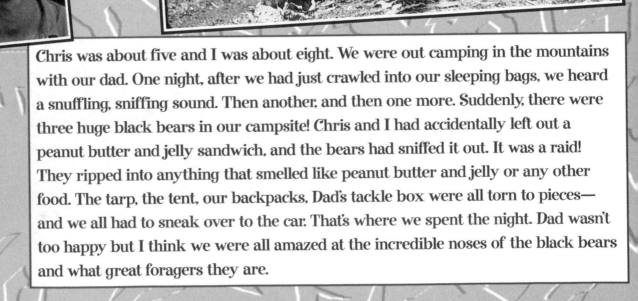

Chris was about five and I was about eight. We were out camping in the mountains with our dad. One night, after we had just crawled into our sleeping bags, we heard a snuffling, sniffing sound. Then another, and then one more. Suddenly, there were three huge black bears in our campsite! Chris and I had accidentally left out a peanut butter and jelly sandwich, and the bears had sniffed it out. It was a raid! They ripped into anything that smelled like peanut butter and jelly or any other food. The tarp, the tent, our backpacks, Dad's tackle box were all torn to pieces— and we all had to sneak over to the car. That's where we spent the night. Dad wasn't too happy but I think we were all amazed at the incredible noses of the black bears and what great foragers they are.

Bears are great foragers. That's how they survive. Black bears are omnivores. That means they'll eat plants, vegetables, and animals.

The Black Bear Buffet

Berries, grass (they graze just like cows), fish, roots, bee larvae and honey, grubs, bird eggs, lizards. And a black bear has a very, very big appetite.

During the spring, summer, and fall the bear has to eat enough to get him through the winter. In the winter, a black bear doesn't eat anything. It goes into a lazy state called "winter-sleep" for about five months.

Where does the bear sleep?

In a bear den, which can be in a cave, in a log, under a brush pile, in a hole in the ground, and even under a building. When the bear wakes up in the spring, it is very, very hungry. It will eat anything that smells good. That's why you have to be bear-smart when you're camping.

Bears can be dangerous, so you don't want hungry bears in your campground. This is what you should do when you go camping:

1. Set up your camp.

2. Put all your food in one pack.

3. String it up a tree, and hoist it up and out of the black bear's reach.

That trick works great for bears but there is another one of our favorite creatures who could certainly reach food hanging high in trees. Do you know who we are talking about? Here's a hint: It's the tallest creature on Earth today. You guessed it...

The Giraffe

Giraffes tower above you and the treetops. They are 15–16 feet tall, the tallest animals on planet Earth today !

Of all the grazers in Africa, including wildebeests, zebras, impalas, and gazelles, giraffes are the only animals that can get to the leaves on the tops of trees. That's why they have such long necks!!

Wouldn't people look weird if they had 8-foot-long necks?

But that's only one long thing about giraffes. Long legs also help the giraffe get up to the treetops.

A giraffe has an 18-inch-long tongue!

The giraffe's long tongue helps it to gather leaves. Look at how this giraffe uses its tongue and lips to pick leaves from a thorn-filled branch.

Have you ever tried sneaking up on a giraffe? When we were in Botswana, we spent a whole day trying. But it just can't be done. A giraffe sees *everything* around him. A giraffe always spotted us before we even got close. That's another advantage of a long neck. A giraffe can usually see a lion coming.

When giraffes fight, they slam each other with their necks. We call it neck-knocking.

With such cool features, the giraffe is definitely in the running to be one of our favorite creatures. Hey, wait a minute. What's that behind the giraffe? It's a . . .

Warthog

Who's better-looking,
Chris or the warthog?
Your choice:
warthog ___ Chris ___
Martin's choice:
warthog _X_ Chris ___

Warthogs are tough creatures who survive despite all the odds stacked against them!!
Warthogs live in Africa and every predator on the African savanna is out to get them! That means they have to be on the lookout for leopards, lions, pythons, crocodiles, crowned eagles, hyenas, jackals, cheetahs, honey badgers, and African wild dogs.
They *all* want to eat a warthog!

So how do they survive? Well the warthogs have some good tricks and traits to help them escape from predators. One of these is courage! A warthog is one brave pig!

Luckily a warthog has slashing tusks! No predator goes after a warthog without risk. Warthog tusks are razor-sharp. They slash with the lower ones and hook up with the top ones. (By the way, warthog tusks are special teeth.) Their faces are hard like rocks and the warts absorb the impact when they head-butt.

When they have to run, Mom raises her tail. They follow her tail, which is sticking up in the air through the long grass! This is how a mom warthog leads her babies to safety.

And when they are on the run, they use the old back-into-the-hole defense. A warthog backs into its burrow, blocking the entrance with its hard head and sharp tusks!
If you think a warthog is cute, you'll really like the…

Bent-Wing Bat

You have to go to the Mt. Etna Bat Caves in Australia if you want to see bent-wing bats. But take our word for it, it's worth the trip!

During our bent-wing bat adventure, we climbed up the mountain until we reached the cave entrance. The cave entrance was surrounded with sharp, pointed rock. We had arrived before dark—just in time for the great bent-wing bat spectacle!! All we had to do was wait at the cave entrance until dark. And that's when we saw...

The Great Bent-Wing Emergence!!

As the sun went down, the bats began to stir down in the cave. The night belongs to the bats!

Before we saw any bats, we felt a cool breeze coming from the cave. There were so many bats flying around in there that they were making their own windstorm!

Finally, they started coming. Bats, bats, and more bats! They just kept pouring out of the cave! We thought it would never end! There were a quarter of a million—that's 250,000—bats!

But those bats didn't have an easy time getting out of the cave. We weren't the only ones waiting for the bats at the cave entrance. There were some predators waiting... some *serious* predators.

- **Pythons** stretch themselves out into the opening of the cave and snatch bats in midair!

- **Giant tree frogs** can swallow a bent-wing bat whole!

- **Falcons** swoop down and catch bats with their sharp talons!

- **Owls** are great night hunters.

- **Ghost bats**: These bats are big! And they like to hunt bent-wing bats!

Luckily, plenty of bent-wing bats outmaneuvered these predators and flew off into the night to hunt!

Bent-wing bats love to eat mosquitoes. And boy can these bats pack them in! A bent wing bat can eat about 3,000 mosquitoes in a single night!!

Could you eat 3,000 hamburgers in one day?

The Bent-Wing Bat Mosquito Detector—Echolocation!

This is how it works:

1) The bat makes a sound with its throat. The sound is so high-pitched that humans can't even hear it!

2) The sound bounces off the mosquito and heads back toward the bat.

3) The bat hears the returning sound with his super-sensitive ears. Judging by how long the sound took to get back to him, he can tell where the mosquito is. The longer it takes the sound to get back, the farther away the mosquito.

4) The bat flies to mosquito and munches him.

5) On to the next mosquito!!!

Bat Wing

Human Hand

Bats are great fliers... and it's all in the hands! If you look closely at a bat's wing, you can see that it is actually a hand with skin stretched between the fingers. Wow!!

Before the sun comes up in the morning, the bent-wing bats have returned to their cave — it's their home in the mountain. This is what it looks like:

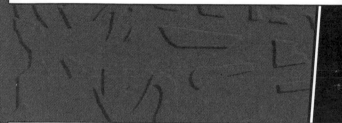

A Look Inside a Bat Cave

- 6-foot deep pool of bat guano on cave floor: Bat guano is bat poop. Some people actually harvest bat poop to use as fertilizer.

- Adult roosting places: Adult bats sleep here during the day.

- Nursery area: This is the part of the cave where bat babies and their moms stay.

- Cave shape: perfectly shaped with a domed roof and the right ventilation; helps keep the cave at the perfect temperature for raising baby bent-wing bats.

- 250,000 bat bodies: They keep the cave heated.

Fruit Bat

The cave is perfect for raising baby bent-wing bats. Bent-wing bats are carried around by their mothers until they are about 12 weeks old. Then they head off on their own.

There are all kinds of cool bats—tube-nosed bats, fruit bats, grey bats, vampire bats…. Wait a second, what about…

The Wombat

Wombat

Hairy-Nosed Wombat

Wombats *aren't* bats... but they *are* really awesome creatures!

Wombats live in Australia — The Land of Marsupials.

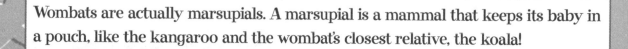

Wombats are actually marsupials. A marsupial is a mammal that keeps its baby in a pouch, like the kangaroo and the wombat's closest relative, the koala!

A wombat is hardly developed when it is born. It's only the size of a bean and goes straight to its mother's pouch.

When it's five months old, it starts to grow fur, and its eyes open.

At 8 months old, it's ready for its first trip outside of the pouch and into the real world!

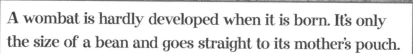

Wombat Menu
Wombats are grazers. They eat grass and moss… and that's it!!

Dingo

Wombats are considered the smartest marsupials of all. Judging by how they deal with predators like the dingo, I'm not surprised!

The Patented "Anti-Dingo" Wombat Rump Shield
(Rump Shield: special pelvic bone used for protection)

Operating Instructions:

- When dingo is after you, head straight for your burrow!

- Go inside as quickly as possible.

- If dingo sticks his head in or tries to dig you out, use your bony rump plate as a shield.

- If dingo persists, put dingo's head between your rump shield and the top of burrow, and…

- Press.

- Warning!!! Wombat rump shields can hurt, and they can even crush dingo skulls!

While we were in Australia, we met an orphaned wombat. She loved to follow us around!

She even sneaked onto our boat when we headed off to Africa! It's a good thing we noticed her and took her back before we went home to North America! Which reminds us of a really *cool* North American canine. We met him in a *cold* place!

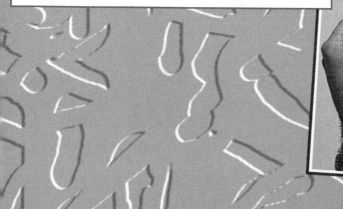

The Wolf

It's kind of weird that this creature that we like so much could be one of the most hated and feared creatures of all time. This drawing gives you a good idea of what people have always thought of wolves.

Chris and Snowball

Martin and Heidi

How could so many people hate wolves when wolves were among the first animals that were friends with humans? Humans domesticated a small type of wolf over 12,000 years ago, and that was probably the first pet dog.

Most of the dogs we know and love today came from the ancestral wolf.

Martin and I wanted to find out what wild wolves were really like so we went up to Alaska to find them. We camped out in the Denali wilderness for weeks. At night, we heard wolves howling in the distance. But we never saw them. Until one day we spotted something moving along a mountain ridge. I whipped out my binoculars and there it was. A wolf. It trotted, gliding across the ridge and then it disappeared into the trees. Wow! We were so happy that we had finally seen a wolf that we didn't notice the wolf materialize out of the woods very close to us. We didn't see it until it was already walking toward us. It stopped 10 feet away, looked at us, and then wandered off down the side of a stream. Wow!

Wolves are not animals to be afraid of. They're just misunderstood. Sort of like another creature we know and love. Some people think it's a scorpion. But it is really a...

Vinegaroon

How could we have forgotten this creature? We just *love* the vinegaroon!

The what!?

The vinegaroon! A.K.A. (also known as) the whip scorpion.

The vinegaroon sprays her enemies with ACID! She has a sac of vinegarlike acid in her tail that she sprays into predators eyes!

The VINEGAROON UNDER ATTACK!

VINEGAROON WAS SITTING QUIETLY IN THE SHADE OF HIS LOG, WAITING OUT THE BLISTERING HEAT OF THE DAY...

SUDDENLY, THE SHELTER IS RIPPED OUT FROM ABOVE!

ROOTS BREAK AROUND HIM! EARTH AND CHUNKS OF BARK CRASH TO THE GROUND!

IT'S COATI!!! WITH HIS SHARP DIGGING CLAWS, QUICK MOVEMENTS, AND SHARP TEETH, COATI IS ONE OF VINEGAROON'S MOST FEARED FOES!

COATI STRIKES WITH A QUICK RIGHT PAW!

VINEGAROON DODGES LEFT IN THE NICK OF TIME!

VINEGAROON WASTES NO TIME. HE CALLS UPON HIS SECRET WEAPON.

HEE HEE

LIFTING HIS WHIP TAIL, HE...

...AIMS DIRECTLY AT COATI'S EYES...

PSST!

...AND SPRAYS!

YEOW!

This is the secret formula for vinegaroon acid. Vinegaroon acid is similar to vinegar, the stuff that is in your salad dressing!!

These aren't antennae. They're legs!!! The whip scorpion has super-specialized front legs that it uses in the same way that insects use antennae... for feeling!!

You've heard of fish having gills, right? Well, they're not the only ones! The whip scorpion doesn't live in water, but he actually has gills for breathing, just like a fish!!

Gills! Fish!! That reminds us of the...

Reef Sharks

White-tipped reef shark

This is one incredible fish!

Definitely one of the most amazing experiences we've ever had was when we came face to face with this predator. After all, check out her face!

A reef shark's teeth are razor sharp and serrated—perfect for catching and cutting up prey, like fish!

These sharks always have a mouthful of teeth and the teeth are *always* sharp. In fact, when the front teeth wear out and become blunt, they fall out and are replaced by a brand-new set of teeth that grows in behind them! In her lifetime, this shark will have gone through thousands of teeth—all of them sharp!!

A lot of people are terrified of sharks and their sharp teeth. We weren't terrified. But when we went to the Bahamas to meet the Caribbean reef shark, we weren't quite sure what to expect!

We loaded up our dive boat and headed out to find the sharks. When we reached the place where the sharks were, we put on our scuba gear, made sure we knew our underwater hand signals, and jumped into the sea!

We dove down 50 feet—and that's when we spotted them! They were each about 8 feet long and there were seven of them. Finally, we were face to face with sharks!

Caribbean Reef Sharks

The funny thing was that neither of us were afraid! All we could think about was how beautiful, powerful, ancient, and graceful these caribbean reef sharks were as they glided all around us! Wow! It was incredible!

Even though some sharks can be dangerous they really aren't as scary as people make them out to be! When you think about it, there are approximately 370 different types of shark in the world but only about 6 of them would think of humans as food.

But all 370 are some of the most incredible creatures in the water!

Hey, speaking of water...

Micro Organisms

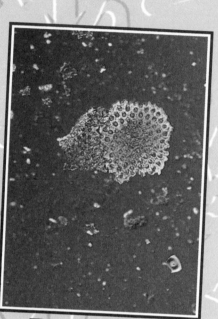
Radiolaria

Amhipod

Paramecium

Green Hydra

If you take a look in a drop of water (even in winter), you'll be amazed at all the little animals swimming around. But you'll need a little help from a microscope to see them. Set it at a really high magnification and...WOW!

"Wait! We're running out of pages!"

What about leopard tortoises, Tasmanian devils, dolphins, chameleons, tarantulas, elephants?? All of these animals could be our favorite creatures, too!

How can we possibly pick a favorite of all these creatures. Every creature you think about has some special feature, talent, or characteristic that puts it right up there in the running. We've really got to think this through.

Hey Martin, you know we've never been to China to check out red pandas or golden snub-nosed monkeys. **Let's go!**